Ohio: A Photographic Portrait 1935-1941
Farm Security Administration Photographs

Carl Mydans
Theodor Jung
John Vachon
Arthur Rothstein
Ben Shahn
Russell Lee
Marion Post Wolcott

Exhibition Organized by Carolyn Kinder Carr
Akron Art Institute, Akron, Ohio

International Standard Book Number: 0-87338-244-7
Library of Congress Catalog Card Number: 80-65227
Published by the Akron Art Institute, Akron, Ohio
Distributed by Kent State University Press, Kent, Ohio
© 1980 Akron Art Institute
Printed by Holsing Lithograph Company, Canton, Ohio
Designed by Cynthia Davidson-Powers

Cover: Arthur Rothstein, *General Store and Railroad Crossing,*
Atlanta, May 1938

Published with the support of The Ohio
Program in the Humanities, a state-based
program of the National Endowment for
the Humanities.

Contents

3

Acknowledgments

Since its invention in 1839, photography, with its unparalleled ability to render reality and arrest a moment in time, has been an important tool of communication and artistic expression. Always a source of scholarly and critical discussion, a burgeoning interest in this medium since the 1960s has precipitated further examination of photography's various traditions and the work of major photographers.

A conversation with John Coplans, former director of the Akron Art Institute, about the various kinds of photography and prominent personalities associated with the medium, led to this exhibition. While speaking of the history of socially committed photography, which reached its apogee during the 1930s with the implementation of the government-sponsored Farm Security Administration (FSA) photographic survey, it became apparent to me that the FSA photographs taken in Ohio between 1935 and 1941 had never been examined as a cohesive entity.

This exhibition and accompanying catalogue have been realized with the generous assistance of numerous persons and institutions. A grant from the Ohio Program in the Humanities provided major funding for this project. This grant permitted me to travel to Washington, D.C., in order to examine the FSA photographic archive in the Prints and Photographs Division of the Library of Congress, to select and purchase the works for this exhibition, and to read unpublished interviews with the FSA photographers at the Archives of American Art. The grant also partially supports this catalogue as well as a public symposium to be held 13 April 1980 at the Akron Art Institute. The Statewide Arts Services Program of the Ohio Foundation of the Arts, Inc., is circulating the exhibition to other museums and institutions throughout Ohio.

I am grateful to my three collaborators whose catalogue essays have placed these FSA photographs within a broader historical context. While I have written on the genesis and direction of the survey and on the styles and assignments of the individual photographers who came to Ohio, Dr. Lewis Fried, Kent State University, has discussed parallel trends in '30s documentary literature; Dr. Bernard Sternsher, Bowling Green State University, has identified the government programs which sought to rectify the social and economic problems depicted in the photographs; Dr. David Kyvig, The University of Akron, has pointed out the need to interpret these photographs in relation to other kinds of historical data.

I am indebted to Russell Lee, Arthur Rothstein, and Marion Post Wolcott for permission to read their interviews at the Archives of American Art, Washington, D.C. Carl Mydans also supplied me with unpublished information from his personal notebooks, while Theodor Jung sent me otherwise inaccessible data about his career. Davis Pratt, curator of photography, The Fogg Museum, Harvard University, gave me access to the Ben Shahn archive, enabling me to compare their FSA prints with those by Shahn in the Library of Congress FSA archive. David Horvath, curator of the photographic archives, University of Louisville, kindly provided relevant information from the Roy Stryker archive at that institution.

I wish to thank Patricia Anderson, who typed the catalogue manuscript; Cynthia Davidson-Powers, Akron Art Institute public information officer, who designed the catalogue and provided, along with Marcianne Herr, Akron Art Institute curator of education, invaluable editorial assistance.

C.K.C.

The Farm Security Administration Photographic Survey

Genesis and Direction

A remarkable pictorial document of American society in the years 1935-1943 is preserved in the Prints and Photographs Division of the Library of Congress. This photographic archive, consisting of more than 170,000 negatives and 70,000 prints, was commissioned by the Resettlement Adminsitration, known after its reorganization in 1937 as the Farm Security Administration (FSA).[1]

The direction and character of the Farm Security Administration photographic survey was shaped by Roy Emerson Stryker (1893-1975). In July 1935 Stryker was hired as chief of the Historical Section of the Information Division of the Resettlement Administration by Rexford Guy Tugwell. Tugwell, former economics professor at Columbia University, Roosevelt "brain truster," Assistant Secretary of Agriculture, and head of the Resettlement Administration, sought a photographic documentation of rural problems to demonstrate to Congress and the American people the scope and success of the Resettlement Administration's programs. Tugwell was well aware of the persuasive power·of photography for he had used photographs to illustrate his highly successful book, *American Economic Life*.[2]

Stryker's job was broadly defined:

to direct the activities of investigators, photographers, economists, sociologists, and statisticians engaged in the accumulation and compilation of reports, statistics, photographic material, vital statistics, agricultural surveys, maps, and sketches necessary to make accurate descriptions of the various phases of the Resettlement Administration with particular regard to the historical, sociological, and economic aspects of the several programs and their accomplishments.[3]

As chief of the Historical Section, Stryker's genius was twofold: he hired young, unknown, but exceptionally talented photographers; he transformed the scope of the photographic survey from an instrument of pure data and propaganda into a chronicle of American life.

By the mid-1930s, when Stryker began the survey, government-sponsored photographic surveys and the use of photographs as instruments of political action were not new concepts. As early as 1867 the United States government commissioned Civil War photographer Timothy O'Sullivan to accompany Clarence King's geological survey of the 40th parallel, an expedition which, like subsequent surveys employing photographers, was vital to the development of the American West. In the 1890s the publication of Jacob Riis' *How the Other Half Lives*, a photographic study of New York's Lower East Side slums, was a significant force in mitigating various abuses of the poor. Similarly, the child labor photographs of Lewis Hine, commissioned in 1908 by the National Child Labor Committee, served as a catalyst for subsequent legislative reforms.

Moreover, Stryker and Tugwell's understanding of the effectiveness of photography as a tool of mass communication and its potential to instantly and succinctly convey the nature of the human condition was neither a unique nor isolated phenomenon. The '30s was an era which witnessed the burgeoning of photojournalism, a fact reflected and enhanced by the founding of the American picture magazines, *Life* (1936) and *Look* (1937). Similarly, the documentary approach, ostensibly a dispassionate gathering of observed data without editorial comment, permeated myriad fields of creative and scholarly endeavor in the '30s, including fiction, films, theatre, dance, economics, history, and sociology.[4]

The FSA photographic survey was thus both a product and a symbol of the era. It was distinguished, however, by its scale, its scope, and the consistent quality of its imagery. Never before had any photographic survey, public or private, brought together so many socially concerned photographers. Never had a government agency been willing to commission images of its poverty as well as its prosperity. The goal of the photographers was advocacy: initially for political reform; ultimately for the dignity, strength, and courage of the American people. Unlike most government-sponsored photographers, the FSA photographers were not interested in heroes and historic events in the traditional sense; unlike photojournalists, they were not concerned with the unusual or the grotesque. Instead, they sought to record the ordinary and render it extraordinary.

Walker Evans, Dorothea Lange, Carl Mydans, Theodor Jung, Arthur Rothstein, John Vachon, Marion Post Wolcott, Russell Lee, Ben Shahn, John Collier, and Jack Delano were among the photographers who worked for Stryker between the program's inception in 1935 and Stryker's resignation in 1943.[5] Stryker was intimately involved in the work of each of these photographers. He insisted they be familiar with the social, geographical, political, and historical characteristics of the areas to be visited.[6] Stryker also made the final selection of photographs to be placed in the FSA file.[7]

In September 1936 Stryker met with Robert Lynd, author of the famous sociological study *Middletown* (1929).[8] This meeting was crucial in expanding the perimeters of the FSA survey. From it emerged a "script," a list of more than 200 items detailing every aspect of daily life in a small town (Appendix). Subsequently an increasing number of FSA photographs focused on middle-class life rather than solely on the problems of the poor and the achievements of the Resettlement Administration's programs. What remained constant, however, was the sense of moral commitment. As Arthur Rothstein stated:

> I think we had a great social responsibility. We were dedicated to the idea that our lives can be improved, that man is the master of his environment and that it is possible for us to live a better life, not only materially, but spiritually as well . . . . We were all inspired with a kind of missionary zeal, a dedication for social improvement.[9]

Of the photographers who worked for Stryker, only Carl Mydans, Theodor Jung, John Vachon, Arthur Rothstein, Ben Shahn, Russell Lee, and Marion Post Wolcott were sent to Ohio in the years before World War II. Each was given a slightly different assignment: Mydans photographed the slums of Cincinnati; Jung, the life of the rural hill people in Ross and Jackson counties; Vachon, primarily the street life of Cincinnati and the American ideal of suburban living. Rothstein was particularly interested in the psychological and social implications of the changing seasons. Shahn, assigned to cover the harvest in central Ohio, captured the rich abundance of the farm land, the integrity of the hard-working farmers and the quiet intimacy of small-town social life. Lee's work was limited to construction views of Greenhills, a planned community designed for the Suburban Resettlement Administration. Post Wolcott only photographed farms in the vicinity of Dayton.

Many images taken on assignment for the FSA, such as Dorothea Lange's *Migrant Mother* and Arthur Rothstein's *Dust Storm, Cimarron County, Oklahoma,* are a standard part of America's visual iconography.[10] The Ohio FSA photographs are less well-known; they have been published only sporadically and have never been exhibited previously as a cohesive group.

The more than 100 prints in this exhibition represent only a fraction of the approximately 3,000 photographs taken in Ohio for the FSA, yet they provide a synopsis of the work done in Ohio, revealing the nature of the specific assignments and reflecting the individual styles of the photographers.

These photographs provide, for the present, a vision of life in Ohio in the waning years of the Depression. They remind us that, while prices have changed, social interaction in a small town has not. They suggest that, compared to conditions in the South, in the Oklahoma Dustbowl, and among migrant laborers in California, the poverty in Ohio was neither as intense nor as pervasive. These photographs represent only a fraction of a limitless reality; nevertheless, unique and unparalleled insights lie within this visual microcosm.

Carolyn Kinder Carr
Curator of Art
Akron Art Institute

1. Several monographs discuss the Farm Security Administration photographic survey, among them: Edward Steichen, ed., *The Bitter Years, 1935-1941: Rural America as Seen by the Photographers of the Farm Security Administration* (New York: Museum of Modern Art, 1962); F. Jack Hurley, *Portrait of a Decade: Roy Stryker and the Development of Documentary Photography in the Thirties* (Baton Rouge: Louisiana State University Press, 1972); Roy Emerson Stryker and Nancy Wood, *In This Proud Land: America 1935-1943 as Seen in the FSA Photographs* (Greenwich: New York Graphic Society, 1973); Hank O'Neal, *A Vision Shared: A Classic Portrait of America and Its People 1935-1943* (New York: St. Martin's Press, 1976).

2. Rexford G. Tugwell, Thomas Munro and Roy E. Stryker, *American Economic Life* (New York: Harcourt, Brace, and Company, 1935). Stryker was both a student and colleague of Tugwell in the economics department at Columbia University. It was as photography editor for this innovative text that Stryker developed an interest in photography and became aware of its tremendous impact in formulating public opinion (Hurley, *Portrait of a Decade*, pp. 8-16; Stryker and Wood, *In This Proud Land*, pp. 10-11).

3. Hurley, *Portrait of a Decade*, p. 36; Stryker and Wood, *In This Proud Land*, p. 11.

4. William Stott, *Documentary Expression and Thirties America* (London, Oxford, New York: Oxford University Press, 1973).

5. Hurley, *Portrait of a Decade*, p. 164 ff. By March 1942 the focus of the Farm Security Administration survey had changed radically. Not only was it subject to budget cuts, but much of its work was for the Office of War Information. No Farm Security Administration photographers were assigned to Ohio after 1941 except John Vachon, who, in 1943, came briefly for the Office of War Information.

6. Stryker and Wood, *In This Proud Land*, p. 13.

7. Ibid., p. 17. In all, 270,000 photographs were taken for the Farm Security Administration survey. Stryker punched holes in approximately 100,000 negatives that he did not consider suitable for the file, an act which has subsequently generated controversy.

8. Hurley, *Portrait of a Decade*, pp. 95-98; Robert S. Lynd and Helen M. Lynd, *Middletown: A Study in Contemporary American Culture* (New York: Harcourt, Brace, and Co. 1929).

9. Interview, Arthur Rothstein with Richard K. Doud, 25 May 1964, Archives of American Art, Washington, D.C., p. 19.

10. Stryker and Wood, *In This Proud Land*, pls. IX, 184.

Related Historical Data

Historians always work from fragmentary remains. Most often only verbal and statistical descriptions survive. To the historian, a photograph can be an unmatchable treasure providing an actual look at the past, in this case the appearance of people affected by the Depression, the atmosphere of a lunch room or a working-class home, and the ambience of farms, housing projects, and main streets.

Photographs have greatly enriched our understanding of conditions, events, and people for more than a century. Yet a photograph, like any other document, represents only one viewpoint at one instant. It may be as ambiguous, misleading, or even biased as any other document. Even a superb image frozen in a Farm Security Administration photograph does not allow us to assume that the entire society looked the same, nor does it explain the causes and processes of change over time. The FSA cameras did not capture a balanced or complete picture of American society in the Depression. Rather, they recorded what Alfred Kazin called "endless fractions of reality."[1] Approached as historical records, the photographs must be considered carefully, for only by evaluating and considering **all** available evidence can the historian responsibly reconstruct the past.

The FSA photographs of Ohio in the late 1930s provide vivid and instructive fractions of reality. In Ohio as elsewhere, FSA photographers concentrated on rural and small-town conditions. Their cameras caught farmers working their fields, attending auctions and fairs, parking their automobiles and buggies along main street. As accurate and telling as these scenes of people may be, by the 1930s only about 15 percent of Ohio's nearly seven million residents lived on farms; another 25 per-

cent lived in towns of fewer than 10,000 people. Forty percent of the people lived in the state's eight largest cities, and the Depression hit them much harder than it hit farmers. In a 1937 survey, unemployment in rural and small-town Ohio stood at around 12 percent, in cities of 10,000 to 100,000 people it was 13.5 percent, but in the eight major cities it averaged 20.5 percent, ranging from 14.7 percent in Dayton to 23.7 percent in Cleveland. Industrial workers, skilled, semiskilled, and unskilled, accounted for 59 percent of Ohio's unemployment while persons who worked on farms accounted for four percent. Emergency government jobs with the Works Progress Administration, Civilian Conservation Corps, or other agencies provided work for only about one-fourth of Ohio's unemployed.[2] Only a few FSA photographs of Cincinnati suggest the bleakness of conditions in urban slums as unemployed workers and their families struggled to manage with only sporadic wages and little assistance from an inadequate relief system. Glimpses of the upper end of the social spectrum are even rarer. A few well-dressed spectators at Cincinnati's sesquicentennial parade and occasional scenes of comfortable, middle-class, residential streets are all that we see to remind us that the majority of urban dwellers remained employed. The state's overall unemployment rate of 15.3 percent in 1937, while deplorable, still meant that more than five out of six people in the labor force had jobs.

The FSA Ohio photographs show, again and again, tired and strained faces. The protraits taken by Theodor Jung, Carl Mydans, Arthur Rothstein, Ben Shahn, and John Vachon cumulatively leave an impression of a stoic society. The people who stare into the camera, slouch on street corners, sit in Cincinnati's Fountain Square, or stand in relief lines seem resigned rather than outraged by their shared suffering. The FSA cameras captured this somber, accepting mood wherever they pointed, making a strong case that such an atmosphere was widespread. But just as the nature and degree of hardship varied, so did reactions. Ohio repeatedly witnessed vigorous protest against prevailing conditions. Industrial workers in Akron, Toledo, Youngstown, and elsewhere manifested their discontent through strikes, sit-downs, and picket lines. Violence flared on numerous occasions. Such angry responses are not to be seen in these photographs, which otherwise provide a compelling vision of individual reactions to the Depression.

Although not even the large FSA photography project could capture the full range of Ohio's conditions and moods, it did underscore dramatically a basic Depression reality: whatever one's personal circumstances, hardship was never distant. The society was affected not only by actual deprivation but also by uneasiness bred of awareness that disaster lurked nearby and could strike anyone, anytime. The camera no doubt heightened such knowledge. A fundamental pessimism and caution gripped the society. For instance, as several photographs show, America's two-decade-old love affair with the automobile continued, but people hesitated to buy new cars. In 1929, Americans purchased 4,455,000 new cars, but during the following decade only an average of 2,142,000 new automobiles were sold per year. However, people drove more than ever during the Depression decade. Although the number of cars on the road had increased by only one-seventh by 1939, gasoline consumption had increased by one-fourth. Hard times may have led to deferral of purchases and other cutbacks in lifestyle, but Americans proved unwilling or unable to forego use of their automobiles.[3]

In a more fundamental manifestation of Depression psychology, people married less frequently, divorced more often, and produced children at a slower rate than in any previous decade in American history. The United States population grew by an average of 13.9 percent per decade from 1900 to 1970, but during the 1930s it grew by only 7.3 percent. In the worst year of the Depression, 1933, there were only 16.6 live births per 1,000 population nationally, and in Ohio only 14.1. Ohio's birth rate of 15.6 for the decade, well below the national average of 17.4, gave perhaps the clearest indication of a basic lack of confidence in the future.[4] Not until the United States became embroiled in World War II did its economy and birth rate regain the vigor they both had displayed before the Depression.

If we do not demand too much from the FSA photographs, they can help us understand the 1930s. They vividly show the conditions of life for many people, and they capture the bleakness which affected the spirits of others. If we balance their eloquent images with other historical knowledge, the FSA photographs can enhance our sense of Ohio society during the Depression.

David E. Kyvig
Department of History
The University of Akron

1. Alfred Kazin, *On Native Ground: An Interpretation of Modern American Prose Literature* (New York: Reynal and Hitchcock, 1942). p. 496.

2. These figures are based on data in U.S., Bureau of the Census, *Census of Partial Employment, Unemployment, and Occupations: 1937*, vol. 3, (Washington: Government Printing Office, 1938): 71-97.

3. U.S., Bureau of the Census, *Historical Statistics of the United States, Colonial Times to 1957* (Washington: GPO, 1960): 362, 462.

4. U.S., Bureau of the Census, *Vital Statistics of the United States, 1944* (Washington: GPO, 1946), 2-3.

Federal Relief Programs

Developments in Ohio should command the attention of anyone interested in the Great Depression because the economic collapse hit the Buckeye state hard: in early 1933 Ohio, together with Illinois, New York, and Pennsylvania, accounted for more than a third of the families on unemployment relief in the United States.

For farmers the Depression began in 1921 with a devastating collapse of farm prices. By 1935, when government-sponsored photographers began to visit Ohio, the producers of staples such as corn and wheat had benefited from the price-support programs of the Agricultural Adjustment Administration (AAA), an agency established in 1933, and farm auctions were far less frequent than they had been in the early days of the Depression. Tenants, sharecroppers, migrant workers, and small subsistence farmers, however, benefited little, if at all, from the AAA, and in 1935, by executive order, President Franklin D. Roosevelt created the Resettlement Administration to deal with the problems of agricultural folk who were not staple farmers.

In December 1936 the Resettlement Administration was transferred to the Department of Agriculture. In September 1937 it was renamed the Farm Security Administration, having received statutory authorization under the Bankhead-Jones Farm Tenant Act of July 1937. In 1946 the Farmers' Home Corporation Act eliminated the FSA while retaining some of its activities: a 40-year tenant farm purchase program and rehabilitation loans to poor, small farmers.

The activities of the FSA, complex and controversial, were concerned with poor people and poor land.[1] Poor people needed emergency aid; poor land required long-range conservation measures. In 1936 there were 650,000 farm families on 100 million acres of poor land. It was necessary either to make the poor land better or to persuade and help the farmers to move to better land. The farming of poor land hurt the agricultural economy. When farm prices rose, farming on poor land increased, undermining the more efficient producers' position in the supply-demand situation. When farm prices fell, farmers on submarginal lands, without purchasing power and unable to pay taxes, required constant, sizable expenditures by local and national governments. Thus the FSA's Land Utilization Division intended to "retire" this land after purchases from voluntary sellers and turn it to non-agricultural uses: wildlife preserves, recreation facilities, Indian reserves, pasturage, and reforestation. In the end, the Farm Security Administration retired only about nine million acres.

The Rural Resettlement Division assisted the sellers in establishing themselves on new land. It also administered a number of subsistence homestead projects inherited from other agencies—28 from the Federal Emergency Relief Administration and 65, of which the FSA completed 34, from the Division of Subsistence Homesteads of the Department of the Interior—and the 34 projects initiated by the FSA itself. One subsistence homestead community turned over to the FSA was Dayton Homesteads. Rexford Tugwell, FSA administrator in 1935-1936, however, did not subscribe to the back-to-the-land idea of the subsistence homestead enthusiasts, who envisioned the settlement of many urban as well as rural people in communities combining subsistence farming with self-help cooperatives and outside employment.

The most publicized activity of the FSA was the construction by the Suburban Resettlement Division of garden or greenbelt cities: Greenbelt, Maryland, near Washington; Greendale, near Milwaukee; Greenhills, near Cincinnati. Although only three of the 25 greenbelt cities originally planned were built, in later years these projects were hailed by experts in city planning as outstanding demonstrations of future possibilities in city development.[2]

While the Suburban Resettlement Division received the most publicity, the Rehabilitation Division accounted for most of the FSA's outlay of funds under its program of financial assistance—loans, grants, debt adjustments—and technical or educational assistance. In the years 1936-1943, this division made $778 million in original loans (averaging $412) and supplemental loans (averaging $202) to 950,000 families. The repayment rate was 86 percent on the amount due as of February 1943.

In time, direct (or market-basket, home, or dole) relief was replaced for employables by the work-relief programs of the Civil Works Administration, 1933-1934, and the Works Progress Administration (WPA), 1935-1943. The relief program in Ohio occasioned a bitter battle between the Roosevelt administration and Governor Martin Davey. WPA head Harry Hopkins launched an investigation which revealed Davey's politicization of relief, and in 1935 relief in Ohio was federalized. By 1938 conditions had improved, and tourism, a visit to an amusement park, or ownership of a car was possible. Unemployment, to be sure, had only been reduced by half from 1933 to the fall of 1937 (more than that if the Bureau of Labor Statistics had not considered workers on work-relief projects to be unemployed), and while there was a severe recession from the fall of 1937 to the spring of 1938, by the summer of 1938, with the resumption of deficit spending and increased defense production, recovery was again underway.

Although the FSA photographs focus primarily on rural America, deprivation also occurred in the major cities. The photographs do not show the organization and activity of labor unions and tumultuous labor-management relations. Ohio was the scene of major, often violent strikes, including the Toledo Auto-Lite strike in 1934, the Toledo Chevrolet strike in 1935, the Akron Goodyear strike in 1936, and the Little Steel strike in northeastern Ohio in 1937, as well as a coal miners' strike in rural southeastern Ohio in 1932 and an onion workers' strike in northwestern Ohio in 1934.

The rank-and-file strikers were not radicals. They did not want to overthrow the capitalist system; they simply wanted a bigger piece of the capitalist pie. Nor were Americans, in general, radical during the Depression. The parade watchers at Cincinnati's sesquicentennial celebration in 1938 reflect a theme historians of the 1930s have emphasized: Americans, despite the hardships they endured, the slowness of recovery, and their sense of betrayal by a selfish, irresponsible elite, nevertheless did not believe there was anything fundamentally wrong with the American people or the American Way.

Bernard Sternsher
Department of History
Bowling Green State University

1. The account of the objectives and activities of the Resettlement Administration and the Farm Security Administration is drawn from Bernard Sternsher, *Rexford Tugwell and the New Deal* (New Brunswick, N.J.: Rutgers University Press, 1964), pp. 262-306. For books, articles, theses, and dissertations concerning Ohio in the 1930s, see the titles cited in the notes in Bernard Sternsher, "Depression and New Deal in Ohio: Lorena A. Hickok's Letters to Harry Hopkins, 1934-1936," *Ohio History* 86 (Autumn 1977): 258-77.

2. For further information on Greenhills, see Robert B. Fairbanks, "Cincinnati and Greenhills: The Response to a Federal Community, 1935-1939," *Cincinnati Historical Society Bulletin* 36 (1978): 223-41.

Literary Parallels

The significance of the Farm Security Administration photographs is similar to that of much American literature during the Great Depression: the loss of hope in traditional notions of politics, history, and promise. The events of the 1930s forced the American writer to define anew the shape of human nature, the form of a meaningful community, and the concept of a relevant politics. This was a large task in a nation whose culture was a significantly affirmative one: a robust individualism, a sense of the commanding opportunities of capitalism, and a seemingly endless horizon for national influence were the basic themes of a great deal of American popular literature and social thought. Amidst the wreckage of everyday life there seemed to be no national traditions that the American writer could rely upon.

One of the major strengths of the literary imagination is its capacity to fuse personal life with social history, and the most powerful writers of the '30s did so with moment and heft, illuminating the politics of everyday life. The commonplace activities of human life became invested with a larger meaning: the passage from youth to maturity, the erosion of adolescent dreams, and the yearning for a life of significance. These were now depicted as social themes that commented upon and reflected American fables and pieties. What opportunities awaited children of promise during the Depression? What dreams could be satisfied? In a number of cases, American writers depicted the growth of characters by arguing that childhood ambitions born of an earlier time, like America's promise of vast opportunities, were dreams that had to be denied. James T. Farrell's *Studs Lonigan,* Jack Conroy's *The Disinherited,* Edward Dahlberg's *Bottom Dogs,* and Mike Gold's *Jews Without Money*—to name just a few—traced the maturation of their protagonists through years filled with bleakness, disease, and death: the symbolic decay of American capitalism.[1]

Dispiriting situations evoke radical change or yearning for transcendence: the choice between revolution or utopia. In the '30s, Marxism seemed to offer an insightful explanation of the crises of capitalism. No less importantly, the apparent sureness of Russia's economic and political reconstruction validated the predictive power of Marxist-Leninist thought. Whereas few American writers became members of the Communist party, a number of them owed much to the theses of the left. The Marxist insistence upon the relationship between consciousness and labor, the rise of capitalism and the formation of new social institutions, and ideology and freedom, gave the writer a chance to see the brutal conditions of the Depression as more than passing, destructive events. The lines of men seeking work, the increasing number of people on the move, and the transformation of family relationships could now be viewed as portents of a new social order; they marked a turn in the very history of consciousness itself. As a result, the working man, the condition of labor, and the laboring day itself became subjects for the novelist. Books such as Pietro Di Donato's *Christ in Concrete,* Mary Heaton Vorse's *Strike!,* and Albert Halper's *The Foundry,* widened the area of American literature by focusing on such topics.[2]

Economic conditions had quickly shredded belief in a rugged individualism. How could a single individual be successful in a marketplace controlled by monopolies and cartels? Collective action and organization, long the key elements in American labor thought, provided the novelist with a different order of protagonist and strategy. Large numbers of individuals enlarged the novelist's field of vision: their banding together provided more numerous possibilities for describing and analyzing historical conditions than did the single protagonist's struggle. The novelist's deployment of the group would lead the reader to believe that by affirming the hope of community, based upon dignity and integrity rather than exploitation, collective action and unity could withstand the disintegrative impact of capitalism. In *The Grapes of Wrath*, John Steinbeck dealt with the Joad family; in *Pity Is Not Enough, The Executioner Waits*, and *Rope of Gold*, Josephine Herbst portrayed the history of the Trexler family; in *U.S.A.*, John Dos Passos described a number of people swept up in shared historical events.[3]

Whereas much literature of the '30s took the urban milieu as background, it would be a mistake to ignore the American writers' attraction to one of the enduring images of our culture: the farmer and the countryside. The picture of the Jeffersonian farmer, a rational, independent being far from the corruption of the cities, had weathered the politics of Populism and the scathing attacks of Thorstein Veblen, in which the farmer was seen as an exponent of a tempered capitalism. In one of the most important yet reactionary challenges to writers on the left, twelve southerners published a group of essays entitled *I'll Take My Stand*.[4] Industrialization, urbanization, cultural pluralism, progressive education, Marxism — these were the evils that marked our age and characterized the North. The quality of human life had been destroyed by mechanization; reconstruction—and here the South could serve as an example—should be based upon agrarian foundations. The Jeffersonian farmer could be recast in the mold of the southern gentry. The book, stained with overt racism and disreputable theories about human dignity, received the criticism it deserved, but it served to remind the American reader that the problems besetting the nation were more than those of urban economies.

While regionalist thinkers wrote about new social opportunities to be created if distinctive geographical sections were to be recognized as authentically interdependent entitles—witness Lewis Mumford's brilliant *The Culture of Cities*—a host of writers described the way those who farmed in particular sections of the country survived the Depression.[5] Erskine Caldwell, in *Tobacco Road* and *God's Little Acre*, wrote of the pitiable debasement of the farmer by the constricting web of southern industrialization and the lure of easy wealth.[6] James Agee and Walker Evans' *Let Us Now Praise Famous Men* spoke with concern of the hardships of several families who were farming the land and carefully revealed their relationship to a larger milieu.[7] Steinbeck's *In Dubious Battle* focused on the hostilities in Caliornia between migrant workers and the farmer-as-businessman.[8]

The value of literature of the Depression lies in what we choose to affirm about it. Just as the FSA photographs are "documentary" by virtue of their capturing a significant moment in our history, so too is a large body of literature that claimed to have rescued for fiction the "reality" of a mean age. Such a contention can be debated (what writer has not argued that he or she has not depicted the world "as it really is"?), but it ought not to be dismissed. For what we have is a distinctive cultural expression of significant aspects of American life: the nature and ways of getting a living in hard times. Few writers today are as attentive to so vital a problem: the nature of work which creates the world we inhabit, a world we must justify.

Lewis Fried
Department of English
Kent State University

1. James T. Farrell, *Studs Lonigan* (New York: Vanguard Press, 1935); Jack Conroy, *The Disinherited* (New York: Covici Friede, 1933); Edward Dahlberg, *Bottom Dogs* (New York: Simon and Schuster, 1930); Mike Gold, *Jews Without Money* (New York: Liveright, 1930).

2. Pietro Di Donato, *Christ in Concrete* (New York: Bobbs-Merrill, 1937); Mary Heaton Vorse, *Strike!* (New York: Liveright, 1930); Albert Halper, *The Foundry* (New York: Viking Press, 1934).

3.   John Steinbeck, *The Grapes of Wrath* (New York: Viking Press, 1939); Josephine Herbst, *Pity Is Not Enough* (New York: Harcourt, Brace, and Company, 1933), and *The Executioner Waits* (New York: Harcourt, Brace, and Company, 1934), and *Rope of Gold* (New York: Harcourt, Brace, and Company, 1939); John Dos Passos, *U.S.A.* (New York: Harcourt, Brace, and Company, 1937).

4.   Twelve Southerners, *I'll Take My Stand* (New York: Harper and Brothers, 1930).

5.   Lewis Mumford, *The Culture of Cities* (New York: Harcourt, Brace, and Company, 1938).

6.   Erskine Caldwell, *God's Little Acre* (New York: Viking Press, 1933), and *Tobacco Road* (New York: Charles Scribner's Sons, 1932).

7.   James Agee and Walker Evans, *Let Us Now Praise Famous Men* (Boston: Houghton Mifflin Co., 1941).

8.   John Steinbeck, *In Dubious Battle* (New York: Colliers, 1936).

The Photographers and Photographs

Carl Mydans
(b. 1907)

Carl Mydans was the first photographer to visit Ohio. His personal notes indicate that he arrived by train in Cincinnati on 30 November 1935 and left on 6 December. Forbes, Court, and Marvin streets and Easton Avenue were some of the places he worked. He stayed at the Hotel Sinton and paid $2.00 a night for his room.

A native of Boston and a 1930 graduate of Boston University's School of Journalism, Mydans worked part-time as a writer and photographer for various magazines and newspapers in Boston and New York before joining the Resettlement Administration in 1934. He was hired to take photographs for a book (never completed) on suburban redevelopment. In late 1935 he was reassigned to the Historical Section.[1]

No correspondence detailing Mydans' precise assignment in Ohio exists. The photographs suggest, however, that Mydans came to Cincinnati to photograph urban poverty, presumably as a means of justifying the Resettlement Administration's suburban resettlement programs, such as the Greenhills development, a planned community near Cincinnati. Although Mydans photographed the poor, his primary concern was their living conditions. When he photographed a slum neighborhood, each house flanked by an outdoor privy, he captured the pervasiveness of poverty. When he photographed a single suburban house, only partially framed and covered with tar paper, he brought to an individual level the reality of the Depression, the disappearance of economic prosperity and the American dream. In this photograph the simple curtains at the windows tell of man's need to enhance his surroundings, despite destitution. The car in the garage speaks not only of the reality of sub-urban life, but of a fundamental facet of American existence. It visually reiterates the statement made by one woman, interviewed by Robert Lynd for *Middletown* (Muncie, Indiana), who said, "I'll go without food, before I'll see us give up the car."[2]

Frequently Mydans focused on the squalor of poverty through close-up still lifes: a filthy privy; a communal sink with the ironic notice, "PLEASE KEEP THIS ZINK [*sic*] CLEAN"; a trash-laden outdoor water supply. These photographs are powerful comments on the need for radical reforms.

Mydans never returned to Ohio. He left the Historical Section in the fall of 1936 to join the staff of the newly formed *Life* magazine. His subsequent photographic essays, such as those taken during World War II and in Korea, indicate he never lost the social conscience and commitment evident in his Farm Security Administration work.

C.K.C.

1. O'Neal, *Vision Shared*, p. 115.
2. Lynd and Lynd, *Middletown*, p. 256.

Bed and Sitting Room in West End Home, Cincinnati, December 1935

17

Slums, Cincinnati, December 1935

Partly Built House Lacking Water and Sewage Disposal, Cincinnati, December 1935

Tent Squatter, Cincinnati, December 1935

Outside Water Supply on Marvin Street, Cincinnati, December 1935

21

Privy, Cincinnati, December 1935

22

Common Hallway Sink in an Old School House,
Cincinnati, December 1935

23

Theodor Jung
(b. 1906)

Theodor Jung was born in Vienna, Austria, but immigrated to Chicago with his family in 1912. He joined the Historical Section in September 1935 after working a year with the Federal Relief Administration, preparing charts with pictorial statistics on unemployment. He was sent to Ohio in April 1936. He went to Cincinnati to photograph at Greenhills, but most of his photographs were taken while covering the reforestation and rehabilitation projects in Ross, Jackson, and Vinton counties.[1]

Jung's photographs reveal repeatedly how age affects one's response to poverty. Three children dressed in patched, unironed clothes and worn, scuffed shoes and seated on the porch of their log cabin are happy; the spiritually demeaning nature of poverty has not as yet touched their carefree lives to any significant extent. Similarly, three young newsboys who look longingly at sporting equipment are still young enough to be enthralled by the possibilities of owning these wonderful things; they have not been overwhelmed by the difficulties of earning a living. The portrait of a pre-adolescent girl speaks of the pivotal nature of this stage in her life: the doll she holds symbolizes her commitment to the fantasies of childhood; her wary, staring eyes suggest her awareness of a difficult future. With age comes disillusionment: two teenage boys are consummately bored by the limitations of their small-town existence; the lined face of a rehabilitation client's wife reveals her pride, as well as her innate suspiciousness and the harsh struggle of her daily existence.

In his photograph of tree planting Jung transforms a banal subject into an image of endless ritual; in his landscapes he conveys the loneliness and isolation indigenous to the hill country.

These photographs stand in stark juxtaposition to the sense of lush abundance found in Ben Shahn and Marion Post Wolcott's views of the flat plains and gently rolling hills of central Ohio.

Jung left the Historical Section in May 1936, immediately after his trip to Ohio. Not only did Jung disagree with Stryker's insistence on thorough factual knowledge of a geographical area (Jung preferred to make photographs based on an intuitive understanding of a situation),[2] but Stryker thought Jung was not providing a sufficient number of photographs for the time and money spent. Stryker himself noted, however, the photographs Jung did take were memorable.[3]

In 1937 Jung joined the Consumer's Council of the Department of Agriculture; in 1940 he was employed by the War Food Administration. He designed posters, publications, and filmstrips for both agencies and continued to use photographs from the FSA files for this work. Jung left Washington in 1944. He continues to photograph and currently lives in Palo Alto, California.

C.K.C.

1. Hurley, *Portrait of a Decade*, pp. 76-78; O'Neal, *Vision Shared*, pp. 26-27; *USA: 1935-1973: Photographs by Theo Jung* (Vienna: Institute of Graphic Arts, 1975).

2. O'Neal, *Vision Shared*, p. 26.

3. Roy Stryker to Theodor Jung, 13 April 1936, Stryker Archives (microfilm), Archives of American Art, Washington, D.C.

Rehabilitation Client's Wife, Jackson County, April 1936

Three Children from Family of Ten to be Resettled, Chillicothe (Vicinity), April 1936

Rehabilitation Client's Child, Jackson County, **April 1936**

27

Newsboys Admiring Sporting Goods, Jackson, April 1936

Sunday Afternoon, Jackson, April 1936

Ross-Hocking Reforestation Project, Chillicothe (Vicinity), April 1936

Zaleski Reforestation Project, Vinton County, April 1936

John Vachon
(1915-1975)

John Vachon, a Minnesota native, was an unemployed graduate student with a degree in Elizabethan poetry when he was hired to work for the Historical Section as a file clerk in May 1936.[1] Vachon, who had no prior experience as a photographer, became interested in photography after studying the works of Dorothea Lange, Walker Evans, and Ben Shahn in the FSA files. Shahn showed Vachon how to use a Leica, and Evans, who insisted Vachon could only learn photography by using an 8 x 10 view camera, also gave him instruction.[2] Clearly, Vachon was both a keen student and an astute observer.

Vachon was with the Historical Section longer than any other photographer. He made numerous trips to Ohio, first in August 1937, and again in October 1938, September/October 1939, October/November 1940, and June and August of 1941.

Vachon's photographs of Greenhills, of the Hardin County poor, and of Ross County relief recipients appear to be directly related to FSA propaganda-motivated assignments. Although his photograph of men seated, talking, and reading their papers in Cincinnati's Fountain Square (as if at an outdoor men's bar) alludes to the impact of the Depression, most of Vachon's Cincinnati photographs reflect Stryker's expansion of the goals of the survey to include views of Middle America's daily existence. In his photographs of observers at Cincinnati's sesquicentennial parade, Vachon fills the frames with a banker, a cook, a waiter, and a mother and child who, drenched with the sunlight of a warm October day, take a break from their everyday routines. In these photographs one does not need to see the parade to feel the excitement. With *Fire Prevention Week,* Vachon suggests American faith in simple slogans; with his collage of signs in Cleveland he captures the quintessential American mix of commerce and religion.

In 1943 when the Office of War Information absorbed the Historical Section, Vachon joined this agency. He left government service in 1945. He was drafted into the army for a short period and then went to work on the Standard Oil of New Jersey photographic project which Stryker was then directing. In 1948 he began photographing for *Look* magazine. In 1973-1974 he received a Guggenheim Fellowship to photograph in North Dakota. Vachon died of cancer in 1975.[3]

C.K.C.

1. Hurley, *Portrait of a Decade*, pp. 154, 156.
2. O'Neal, *Vision Shared*, pp. 267-268.
3. Brian Vachon, "John Vachon: A Remembrance," *American Photographer* 3(October 1979): 34-75.

Gas Station and Gospel Mission, Cleveland, August 1937

Mr. Lansing and Mr. Coperning, FSA Borrowers, Ross County, October 1940

Residential Street, Greenhills, October 1938

Fire Prevention Week, Cincinnati, October 1938

Fountain Square, Cincinnati, October 1938

Waiter and Chef Watching Sesquicentennial Parade, Cincinnati, October 1938

Woman and Son at Sesquicentennial Parade,
Cincinnati, October 1938

Arthur Rothstein
(b. 1915)

Arthur Rothstein, a New Yorker and former student of Stryker at Columbia University, was the first person Stryker hired to work for the Historical Section. He was employed to set up and supervise the darkroom.[1]

Several similarities exist between the early careers of John Vachon and Arthur Rothstein. Rothstein, like Vachon, had no intention of becoming a photographer when he graduated from college. He became interested in photography while working for the Historical Section in another capacity. The work of Ben Shahn, Dorothea Lange, and Walker Evans also served as a catalyst in the development of his personal style. Reflecting on this, Rothstein stated:

Both Walker Evans and Ben Shahn contributed a great deal to my own development as a photographer because they had very definite approaches. For them it was not just a question of making a picture, but of making a picture that had meaning. They made me aware of the elements that go into photography, that go beyond just the contents of the picture—the elements of style, of individual approach, of being able to see clearly, (of) being able to visualize ideas . . .[2]

Rothstein came to Ohio twice: first in May/June 1938 and again in February 1940. His view of Atlanta, Pickaway County, is a classic presentation of a whistle-stop with its general store that provides the necessities of life for the surrounding farms. His *Hotel Lobby* is a poignant statement about isolation and waiting. Fascinated by the textures and sounds of nature, Rothstein photographed the pervasive stillness of the open countryside, the virgin purity of the crystal-clear snow, the spongy terrain of spring, and the glistening streets in a gentle rainstorm.

Like all FSA photographers, Rothstein wrote frequently to Stryker while on an assignment. In his letter dated 16 February 1940 he tells of the breathtaking chill he found and photographed.

I got the full force of the blizzard just after leaving Clarksburg, West Va. It was quite a struggle to get through to Chillicothe. Then when I did arrive, in the middle of a record snow storm for Ross Co., all the rural roads were impassable. The temperature, too, was way below freezing.

Never have I taken pictures under more difficult conditions. Using snow shoes I traversed the Scioto River Basin, passing over drifts which all but covered the shocks of corn in the lowlands. Because of the below freezing temperatures, it was necessary for me to use two contaxes interchangeably which I kept warm by carrying them in the seat of my pants.

In spite of all these difficulties and with the able cooperation of the county agent who was rather reluctant about exposing himself to the rigorous weather, I got quite a few snow pictures, farm scenes . . .

I initiated George by walking him through a cow barn. The manure was at least a foot deep. I think he now has an appreciation for the rural way of life.[3]

In 1940 Rothstein joined the staff of *Look* magazine. He is currently director of photography for *Parade* magazine.

1. Hurley, *Portrait of a Decade*, pp. 27-28, 40; O'Neal, *Vision Shared*, pp. 21-23.

2. Interview, Arthur Rothstein by Richard K. Doud, 25 May 1964, Archives of American Art, Washington, D.C.

3. Arthur Rothstein to Roy Stryker, 16 February 1940, Roy Stryker Collection, University of Louisville, Photographic Archive, Louisville, Kentucky.

General Store and Railroad Crossing, Atlanta, May 1938

Melting Snow, Utopia, February 1940

43   Melting Snow, Clermont County, February 1940

Rural Road, Ross County, January 1939　　　　　44

Rural Road, Ross County, February 1940

Automobile in Snow Drift, Chillicothe, February 1940   46

Hotel Guests Watching Snow Storm, Chillicothe, February 1940

Ben Shahn
(1898-1969)

Ben Shahn, born in Kovno, Lithuania, grew up in Brooklyn and studied art at the National Academy of Design. Shahn was thirty-two and sharing an apartment with Walker Evans in Greenwich Village when his brother bought him his first camera, a 35mm Leica.[1] Shahn, who found his own sketching inadequate, was interested in photography primarily as an aid to his painting. "Photographs give you those details of form you think you will remember but don't."[2]

Shahn's formal photographic training was scant.

Now, my knowledge of photography was terribly limited. I thought I could ask Walker Evans to show me what to do . . . . One day when he was going off to the Caribbean and I was helping him into his taxi, I said, "Walker, remember your promise to show me how to photograph?"

He said, "Well, it's very easy, Ben. F9 on the sunny side of the street. F45 on the shady side of the street. For 1/20th of a second hold your camera steady"—and that was all. This was the only lesson I ever had. Of course, photography is not so much the technical facility as it is the eye and the decision that one makes about the moment at which one is going to snap.[3]

In 1935 Shahn was employed by the Special Skills Division of the Resettlement Administration to do posters, pamphlets, and murals. In this capacity he made trips to the South, Kentucky, and West Virginia to take photographs as raw data for his work. Stryker, impressed with these photographs, requested copies for the Historical Section files and, in the summer of 1938, hired Shahn to photograph the harvest in Ohio.[4]

Shahn described this trip, the problems it posed for him and his style of working:

In 1938 I went on Stryker's payroll, at about half the salary I was getting before, to cover what he called "The Harvest" in Ohio. It was so completely different from the South and from the mine country. It was neat and clean and orderly, and I didn't think it had any photographic qualities for me. At first I said, "Well, I can't do anything about it." Then one day it sort of came to me. I felt it after about two weeks, so I called Roy and I said, "I'll take the job." I stayed about six weeks with this, and worked just day and night on the scene. It was an entirely different thing. In the South or in the mine country, wherever you point the camera, there is a picture. But here you had to make choices . . . .

There were nice orderly farm houses, nice orderly roads, and so on—without sharecroppers and without the mine shacks. It was a little more difficult, but I think I did what I call a nice job. Not only was it the actual harvest. I wanted to know what they did on Sundays, and I covered a lot of church activities. I wanted to know what they did on Sundays to amuse themselves, and I went out to a place called Buckeye Lake. Then there was the auction of a home which had its tragic overtones—a baby carriage. The children for whom that baby carriage was bought were now grandparents themselves . . . . I looked at it almost like a movie script, except they were stills. I'd first go out and photograph all the signs on telegraph poles and trees announcing this auction, and then get the people gathering, and all kinds of details of them, and then examine the things, and the auctioneer, and so forth.

I used what is called an angle finder . . . . The angle finder lets you look off in another direction when you focus, so it takes away any self-consciousness people have.[5]

As Shahn noted, he approached his Ohio assignment cinematographically. He began his narrative with a broad, sweeping view of the rich, lush landscape, with its tall fields of wheat and corn waiting to be harvested. In the background are the massive, white buildings which house the machinery and animals involved in Ohio's large, outwardly prosperous agri-business. Scenes of neat, tidy, tree-flanked farm houses suggest a calm, noble haven from the heat of the sun and the struggle of the job. From this, Shahn turned to images of the workers at their jobs—cutting corn, threshing wheat, baling hay. These panoramic shots were augmented by close-ups of the workers, allowing the viewer an intimate glance into the character of individuals who shared a common commitment to hard work.

Shahn embellished his farm scenes with photographs of town life and leisure-time activities. In the overviews of street life, the formal strength of his photographs lies in his innate feeling for pattern and rhythmic repetition of forms. In his close-ups, the power of Shahn's photographs resides in his ability to capture the significant gesture. These photographs, often taken, as he indicated, with a right-angle view finder, focus on the nuance of body language or expression which, in a fleeting moment, conveys the essence of human interaction and/or personality.

Shahn supplemented his human drama with a variety of still lifes. Signs were a favorite subject. At Floyd's, where you

could eat and then fill up at the rate of six gallons for a dollar, the collage of signs speaks of an era before Sohio and McDonald's, of an age in which the needs of people were met by individuals, not by highly specialized mass-marketers. The pride as well as need of Americans to form associations and meet in groups, first noted by the 19th century social historian Alexis de Tocqueville, is signified in the sign of the Circleville Rotarians. The morality of Middle America is expressed by the hand-lettered statement, "WE DONT BUY PLASTER PARIS MIRRORS AND TRY TO SELL THEM FOR HAND CARVED. . . ."

After his Ohio trip, Shahn left the Farm Security Administration. Although he continued to use photographs as research aids for his paintings, he ceased his involvement with photography as a primary medium.

C.K.C.

1. Interview, Ben Shahn with Richard K. Doud, 14 April 1964, Archives of American Art, Washington, D.C., in John D. Morse, ed., *Ben Shahn* (New York and Washington: Praeger, 1972), p. 135.

2. John D. Morse, "Ben Shahn: An Interview," *Magazine of Art* 37 (April 1944): 136-141, in Morse, *Shahn*, p. 133.

3. Ibid., p. 135.

4. Ibid., p. 135; O'Neal, *Vision Shared*, pp. 45-47. The photographs indicate Shahn worked within a 50-mile radius of Columbus and photographed in the capital as well as at Ashville, Buckeye Lake, Circleville, Lancaster, Linworth, London, Marysville, Mechanicsburg, New Carlisle, Plain City, Somerset, Springfield, Urbana, Washington Court House, and Worthington. In 1940 a selection of Shahn's Ohio photographs were published in two books: Sherwood Anderson, *Hometown* (New York Alliance Corp., 1940); *The Ohio Guide, American Guide Series* (New York: Oxford University Press, 1940), compiled by workers of the Writers Program of the Works Project Administration in the State of Ohio. Two recent monographs also include a selection of Shahn's Ohio photographs: Davis Pratt, ed., *The Photographic Eye of Ben Shahn* (Cambridge: Harvard University Press, 1975); Margaret R. Weiss, ed., *Ben Shahn Photographer: An Album of the Thirties* (New York: DaCapo Press, 1973).

5. Morse, *Shahn*, pp. 136-137.

Home, Central Ohio, Summer 1938

Hartman Farms, Columbus (Vicinity), Summer 1938

Virgil Thaxton, Farmer, Mechanicsburg (Vicinity), Summer 1938

Virgil Thaxton's Daughters, Mechanicsburg (Vicinity), Summer 1938

Harvest Hand on Virgil Thaxton Farm, Mechanicsburg (Vicinity), Summer 1938

Adjusting Straw Stacker on Grain Separator, Central Ohio, Summer 1938

Member of Wheat Threshing Crew, Central Ohio, Summer 1938

Tying Bundles of Wheat by Hand, Central Ohio, Summer 1938

Cultivating Corn, Central Ohio, Summer 1938

Farmer Resting in His Car, Central Ohio, Summer 1938

Tourist Signs, Central Ohio, Summer 1938

Main Street, Lancaster, August 1938

Wonder Bar, Circleville, Summer 1938

Itinerant Photographer, Columbus, August 1938

Main Street, Saturday Afternoon, London, Summer 1938

Street Scene, Circleville, Summer 1938

Street Scene, Washington Court House, Summer 1938

Street Scene, Circleville, Summer 1938

Relief Clients, Urbana, August 1938

Second-Hand Furniture Store, Springfield, Summer 1938

Main Street, Saturday Afternoon, London, Summer 1938

Cranking Car, Worthington, August 1938

Lunch Room, Columbus, August 1938

Amish Wagons, Plain City, August 1938

Spectators at Fourth of July Celebration, Ashville, July 1938

Wrestling Matches at Fourth of July Celebration, Ashville, July 1938

Buckeye Lake Amusement Park, Columbus (Vicinity), Summer 1938

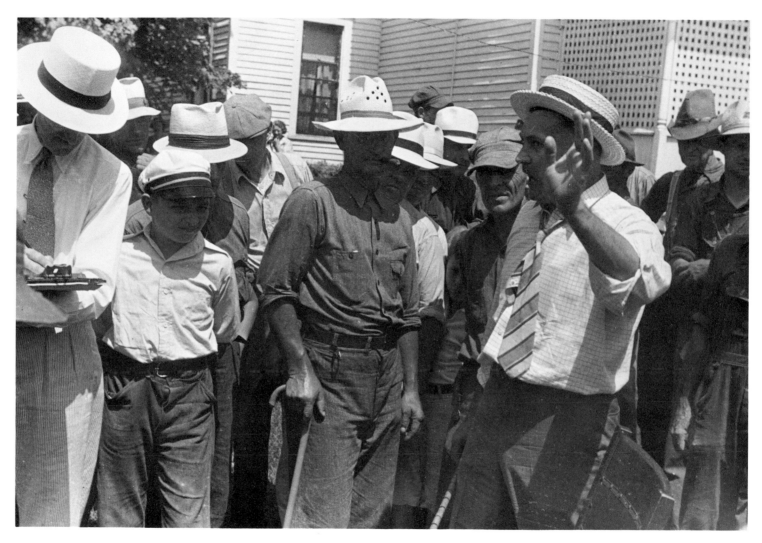

Public Auction, Central Ohio, August **1938**

Spectators at Farm Auction, New Carlisle, Summer 1938

Farmers at Public Auction, Central Ohio, August 1938

Saturday Afternoon on the Other Side of the Tracks, London, Summer 1938

"Hooverville" Children, Circleville, **Summer 1938**

Ex-Farmer Now Employed by the WPA, Central Ohio, August 1938

Sign, Circleville (Vicinity), Summer 1938

Russell Lee
(b. 1903)

Russell Lee, born in Ottawa, Illinois, was graduated in 1925 from Lehigh University with a degree in chemical engineering. In 1929, after working four years for Certainteed Products, Lee left to study painting. He and his first wife, the painter Doris Lee, then went to California, Europe, and in 1931 to Woodstock, New York, to live with the art colony there. In September 1936 Lee joined the Historical Section, replacing Carl Mydans, who had left to work for *Life* magazine.[1]

In October 1936 Lee was given a six-week assignment in the Midwest; he stayed nine months. In February 1937 he photographed the massive flooding along the Ohio and Mississippi rivers. While on this assignment, Lee went to Greenhills and photographed the carpenters, plumbers, and other trades people building this planned community. Most of these photographs are rather pedestrian documents, lacking the insight associated with Lee's photographic essays of Pie Town, New Mexico, and the Blacks in Chicago.

A photograph of a barnyard taken in Hancock County indicates that Lee was also in Ohio in April 1941; in 1942 he left the FSA to take photographs for the Air Force Air Transport Command. In 1946-1947 he was commissioned by the Department of the Interior to photograph for a medical survey of the bituminous coal industry. Subsequently, he worked for Stryker on the Standard Oil of New Jersey photographic survey. In 1947 he moved to Austin, Texas, where he lives today.

C.K.C.

1. F. Jack Hurley, *Russell Lee: Photographer* (Dobbs Ferry: Morgan and Morgan, 1978); O'Neal, *Vision Shared*, pp. 136-138; Hurley, *Portrait of a Decade*, pp. 78 ff.

Workmen Going Home from Work, Greenhills, February 1937

Marion Post Wolcott
(b. 1913)

Marion Post Wolcott, a New Yorker who worked as a staff photographer and feature writer for the *Philadelphia Evening Bulletin,* joined the Historical Section at the end of 1938.[1] She came to Ohio only once, in October 1941. She stayed in the Dayton area and photographed farms. This limited imagery gives no true indication of her abilities as a photographer.

In 1942 Post Wolcott resigned from the Farm Security Administration. She stopped photographing professionally to raise a family and did not resume her serious commitment to photography until 1976. She presently lives in Mendocino, California.

C.K.C.

1. O'Neal, *Vision Shared,* pp. 174-177; Hurley, *Portrait of a Decade,* pp. 108, 110.

Farm, Dayton (Vicinity), **October 1941**

Catalogue of the Exhibition

Carl Mydans

1. Bed and Sitting Room in West End Home
   Cincinnati, December 1935
   LCUSF33-336-M3
2. Slums
   Cincinnati, December 1935
   LCUSF34-2765D
3. Partly Built House Lacking Water and Sewage Disposal
   Cincinnati, December 1935
   LCUSF33-311-M4
4. Tent Squatter
   Cincinnati, December 1935
   LCUSF33-322-M5
5. Outside Water Supply on Marvin Street
   Cincinnati, December 1935
   LCUSF33-321-M5
6. Privy
   Cincinnati, December 1935
   LCUSF33-332-M5
7. Common Hallway Sink in an Old School House
   Cincinnati, December 1935
   LCUSF33-333-M2

Theodor Jung

8. Rehabilitation Client's Wife
   Jackson County, April 1936
   LCUSF33-4100-M1
9. Three Children From Family of Ten to be Resettled
   Chillicothe (Vicinity), April 1936
   LCUSF33-4143-M1
10. Rehabilitation Client's Child
    Jackson County, April 1936
    LCUSF33-4100-M2

11. Rehabilitation Client's House
    Jackson County, April 1936
    LCUSF33-4098-M2
12. Newsboys Admiring Sporting Goods
    Jackson, April 1936
    LCUSF33-4119-M1
13. Sunday Afternoon
    Jackson, April 1936
    LCUSF33-4118-M1
14. Ross-Hocking Reforestation Project
    Chillicothe (Vicinity), April 1936
    LCUSF34-13025C
15. Zaleski Reforestation Project
    Vinton County, April 1936
    LCUSF33-4125-M1

John Vachon

16. Gas Station and Gospel Mission
    Cleveland, August 1937
    LCUSF34-15614-D
17. Mr. Lansing and Mr. Coperning, FSA Borrowers
    Ross County, October 1940
    LCUSF34-61447-D
18. The Lansing Family, FSA Borrowers
    Ross County, October 1940
    LCUSF3-61449-D
19. Daughter of Day Laborer, Scioto Marshes
    Hardin County, November 1940
    LCUSF34-61898-D
20. Day Laborer's House, Scioto Marshes
    Hardin County, November 1940
    LCUSF34-61822-D

21. Swimming Pool, Community Center, Business District
    Greenhills, October 1939
    LCUSF34-60379-D
22. Residential Street
    Greenhills, October 1939
    LCUSF33-1596-M3
23. Children Playing
    Greenhills, October 1938
    LCUSF34-8608-D
24. Fire Station
    Greenhills, October 1938
    LCUSF34-8620-D
25. Fire Prevention Week
    Cincinnati, October 1938
    LCUSF33-1190-M1
26. Fountain Square
    Cincinnati, October 1938
    LCUSF33-1218-M3
27. Flag Passing During Sesquicentennial Parade
    Cincinnati, October 1938
    LCUSF33-1210-M2
28. Waiter and Chef Watching Sesquicentennial Parade
    Cincinnati, October 1938
    LCUSF33-1210-M5
29. Woman and Son Watching Sesquicentennial Parade
    Cincinnati, October 1938
    LCUSF33-1212-M4
30. Downtown Street
    Cincinnati, September 1939
    LCUSF33-1631-M4
31. Residential Street
    Marysville, June 1941
    LCUSF34-62977

Arthur Rothstein

32. General Store and Railroad Crossing
    Atlanta, May 1938
    LCUSF33-2737-M3
33. Melting Snow
    Utopia, February 1940
    LCUSF33-3490-M3
34. Rural Road
    Ross County, February 1940
    LCUSF34-29299-D

35. Melting Snow
    Clermont County, February 1940
    LCUSF33-3487-M3
36. Rural Road
    Ross County, January 1939
    LCUSF34-27085-D
37. Farm
    Ross County, February 1939
    LCUSF33-3493-M5
38. Melting Snow
    Clermont County, February 1940
    LCUSF33-3489-M3
39. Automobile in Snow Drift
    Chillicothe, February 1940
    LCUSF33-3472-M1
40. Popcorn Stand
    Chillicothe, February 1940
    LCUSF33-3473-M1
41. Hotel Guests Watching Snow Storm
    Chillicothe, February 1940
    LCUSF33-3467-M1

Ben Shahn

42. Home
    Central Ohio, Summer 1938
    LCUSF33-6643-M1
43. Hartman Farms
    Columbus (Vicinity), Summer 1938
    LCUSF33-6467-M4
44. Virgil Thaxton, Farmer
    Mechanicsburg (Vicinity), Summer 1938
    LCUSF33-6467-M4
45. Virgil Thaxton Family
    Mechanicsburg (Vicinity), Summer 1938
    LCUSF33-6467-M1
46. Virgil Thaxton's Daughters
    Mechanicsburg (Vicinity), Summer 1938
    LCUSF33-6460-M3
47. Cultivating Corn
    Central Ohio, Summer 1938
    LCUSF33-6433-M4
48. Threshing Wheat
    Central Ohio, August 1938
    LCUSF33-6473-M3

49. Harvest Hand on Virgil Thaxton Farm
Mechanicsburg (Vicinity), Summer 1938
LCUSF33-6504-M3
50. Harvest Hand on Virgil Thaxton Farm
Mechanicsburg (Vicinity), Summer 1938
LCUSF33-6543-M4
51. Adjusting Straw Stacker on Grain Separator
Central Ohio, Summer 1938
LCUSF33-6554-M3
52. Member of Wheat Threshing Crew
Central, Ohio, Summer 1938
LCUSF33-6429-M2
53. Tying Bundles of Wheat by Hand
Central Ohio, Summer 1938
LCUSF33-6486-M1
54. Wheat Threshing Crew
Central Ohio, August 1938
LCUSF33-6554-M1
55. Wheat Harvest Helper Getting Ready for Dinner
Central Ohio, August 1938
LCUSF33-6553-M1
56. Wheat Harvest Helper Getting Ready for Dinner
Central Ohio, August 1938
LCUSF33-6550-M4
57. Farm Wagon
Central Ohio, Summer 1938
LCUSF33-6612-M3
58. Hogs on Thaxton Farm
Mechanicsburg (Vicinity), Summer 1938
LCUSF33-6459-M4
59. Privy on US 40
Central Ohio, Summer 1938
LCUSF33-6563-M3
60. Barn on US 40
Central Ohio, Summer 1938
LCUSF33-6460-M2
61. Farmer Resting in His Car
Central Ohio, Summer 1938
LCUSF33-6468-M2
62. Tourist Signs
Central Ohio, Summer 1938
LCUSF33-6584-M2
63. Main Street
Lancaster, August 1938
I CUSF33-6390-M2

64. Itinerant Photographer
Columbus, August 1938
LCUSF33-6582-M2
65. Wonder Bar
Circleville, Summer 1938
LCUSF33-6632-M2
66. Main Street, Saturday Afternoon
London, Summer 1938
LCUSF33-6537-M5
67. Street Signs
Plain City, August 1938
LCUSF33-6646-M4
68. Street Scene
Circleville, Summer 1938
LCUSF33-6560-M3
69. Main Street, Saturday Afternoon
London, Summer 1938
LCUSF33-6532-M2
70. Street Scene
Marysville, Summer 1938
LCUSF33-6641-M5
71. Street Scene
Circleville, Summer 1938
LCUSF33-6413-M1
72. Street Scene
Washington Court House, Summer 1938
LCUSF33-6407-M1
73. Street Scene
Circleville, Summer 1938
LCUSF33-6415-M1
74. Relief Clients
Urbana, August 1938
LCUSF33-6621-M1
75. Relief Clients
Urbana, August 1938
LCUSF33-6621-M2
76. Store
Washington Court House, Summer 1938
LCUSF33-6572-M1
77. Lunch Room
Columbus, August 1938
LCUSF33-6590-M3
78. Barber Shop Sign
Lancaster, August 1938
LCUSF33-6394-M4

79. Main Street, Saturday Afternoon
London, Summer 1938
LCUSF33-6538-M1

80. Cranking Car
Worthington, August 1938
LCUSF33-6670-M2

81. Used Stoves
Circleville (Vicinity), Summer 1938
LCUSF33-6577-M3

82. Second-hand Furniture Store
Springfield, Summer 1938
LCUSF33-6469-M3

83. Amish Wagons
Plain City, August 1938
LCUSF33-6648-M1

84. Parked Cars Near Race Track
Lancaster, August 1938
LCUSF33-6401-M1

85. Spectators at Fourth of July Celebration
Ashville, July 1938
LCUSF33-6444-M4

86. Wrestling Matches at Fourth of July Celebration
Ashville, July 1938
LCUSF33-6439-M2

87. Buckeye Lake Amusement Park
Columbus (Vicinity), Summer 1938
LCUSF33-6600-M1

88. Spectator, County Fair
Central Ohio, August 1938
LCUSF33-6653-M2

89. Spectators, County Fair
Central Ohio, August 1938
LCUSF33-6650-M3

90. Spectators, County Fair
Central Ohio, August 1938
LCUSF33-6663-M4

91. Public Auction
Central Ohio, August 1938
LCUSF33-6680-M4

92. Farmers at Public Auction
Central Ohio, August 1938
LCUSF33-6684-M4

93. Spectators at Farm Auction
New Carlisle, Summer 1938
LCUSF33-6635-M5

94. Spectators at Farm Auction
New Carlisle, Summer 1938
LCUSF33-6633-M5

95. Farmers at Public Auction
Central Ohio, August 1938
LCUSF33-6674-M3

96. Saturday Afternoon on the Other Side of the Tracks
London, Summer 1938
LCUSF33-6514-M3

97. "Hooverville" Children
Circleville, Summer 1938
LCUSF33-6579-M1

98. "Hooverville" Boy
Circleville, Summer 1938
LCUSF33-6578-M1

99. "Hooverville" Resident
Circleville, Summer 1938
LCUSF33-6628-M3

100. Ex-farmer Now Employed by the WPA
Central Ohio, August 1938
LCUSF33-6574-M3

101. Ex-farmer Employed by WPA
Central Ohio, Summer 1938
LCUSF33-6576-M5

102. Relief Family
Urbana (Vicinity), August 1938
LCUSF33-6625-M4

103. Sign
Circleville (Vicinity), Summer 1938
LCUSF33-6395-M2

Russell Lee

104. Workmen Going Home from Work
Greenhills, February 1937
LCUSF34-10240-E

Marion Post Wolcott

105. Farm
Dayton (Vicinity), October 1941
LCUSF34-90033-D

106. Dairy Cows
Dayton (Vicinity), October 1941
LCUSF34-90039-D

Copies of the photographs in this exhibition may be ordered from the Library of Congress by referring to the LCUSF number given in this catalogue.

Appendix

The Small Town
A check outline for photo-documentation
By Roy E. Stryker
University of Louisville, Roy Stryker Collection

I. On the Street
   A. General views of the main street (or streets). Choose these shots carefully to give an "over-all" sense of the main part of the town.
   B. Buildings (representatives—Close-ups of the more important buildings—these should include whole fronts, windows, and doors.

Stores	Theaters
Churches	Garages
Hotels	Restaurants

     Shops—barber, shoe, etc.
     Public buildings—town hall, jail, court house, (cooler—calaboose), fire house, etc.
    Details of the above—fire escapes, balconies, special signs, details of facades, awnings, etc.
   C. People on the street. Let these be quite representative. The shots should show faces, clothing, and activities.
     Men loafing and talking
     Window shopping   "Saturday afternoon"
     Women and children waiting for the men
     Men and women coming out of stores with bundles and packages—e.g., in country towns men carrying tools and harness out of hardware store
     Women pushing baby carriages
     Crowds crossing at intersections
     Street meetings (unusual)
   D. On the walk—(non-personal)

Sidewalk displays	Fire hydrants
Traffic signs	Curb signs
Crossings	Hitching posts

     Good pictures of tree-lined streets (N.J. elm-lined street)
   E. Street Traffic
     Cars and trucks—parked and in transit
     Wagons and horses   Sprinkler wagons
     Street cleaners
     Loads on or in trucks—to show the nature of the

products grown or produced in the neighborhood, e.g., corn, potatoes, cattle, hogs, cord wood, etc.
Waiting for buses and street cars
Traffic signals

II. Stores

Outside—window displays and signs
These are important as they give some key to the purchasing habits of the inhabitants.
Inside—counters, goods on tables, shelves, and racks.
Note the class of goods on tables, shelves and obtain good photos of characteristic items, e.g., "patent" medicines.
Clerks—close-ups—how they dress
People being served   Posters and other ads
(Make photos in various types of stores)

III. Theaters

Front view—details of ticket booth, displays, person selling tickets—note signs in ticket booths (box office)
Groups buying tickets, looking at displays

IV. Banks

Outside views—people looking out of windows—signs on the windows
Inside views—people working in bank—close-ups.
Interesting views might be obtained showing the activity in a small country bank, e.g., the "banker" interviewimg a farmer.
Equipment

V. Other

Restaurants and cafes
Shots of windows showing menus and "specials" listed on window
Interesting pictures could be obtained inside showing counters, tables, slot machines, cigar cases, menus, and posters on wall
Pictures of groups eating at counters and tables
People who work in restaurant
(get picture of the sign "SHORT ORDER" on restaurant window)
Ice cream parlors   Shoe shops
Barber shops   Drug and hardware stores
Soda counters—clerks and people being served
Notion store   Seed and feed store
Pool halls   Saloons and beer parlors

Funeral parlor
Pictures of funerals—crepe on door—processions—burials
Lumber and fuel yards Second-hand stores
Shining parlors   Harness shops

VI. Hotels

Outside picture
Close-up of people on porch
Cars parked in front
Lobby pictures
Desk   People sitting around (close-ups)
Signs and posters on walls
Dining rooms
Interesting pictures can be taken in small town hotels
Display room where travelling men display their goods.
Watch for a display and get picture of local merchants looking over goods.

VII. Garage

This place has taken the place of the livery stable as the meeting place of the town loafers, the "men-about-town".
Very interesting pictures could be obtained at the garage.
Signs—oil barrels

VIII. The Filling Station

A good set of pictures taken over an interval of time would give some idea of the "life" which passes through the town.
This may also be a "town meeting" place.

IX. The People of the Town at Their Work

Pictures of the people of the town and what they do
Editor of the local paper   Doctor (and his office)
Lawyer (and his office)   Town Marshall or police
Postman or rural mail carrier   Butcher
Plumber   Barber
Druggist filling prescriptions   Blacksmith
Filling station attendant   Harness maker
Clerks   And others

X. Transportation

The railroad station (see special shooting script)
The bus terminal (see special shooting script)
Street cars   Automobiles

XI. Church

People
Going to church   Coming out of church

Visiting after church   Inside photographs
Revivals
Buildings
    The church   The parsonage
    Church schools   Building details

XII. Lodges
    Lodge halls   Signs and window displays
    Lodge celebrations   Lodge parades

XIII. The "Square," The Common
    Anything of special interest such as the bandstand,
    comfort stations, fire bell, bulletin boards.
    A view looking down on the square on Saturday afternoon
    or on special occasions.

XIV. Country Club
    A good set of pictures of the small town country club—
    the people who go to the club—and how they amuse
    themselves.

XV. Recreation
    As complete a record of recreation as is possible
    Baseball—the ball grounds
    Local football
    Children at play, organized and unorganized
    Picnics   Special and local games
    Swimming—"the old swimming hole"

XVI. Special Celebrations
    Farmers picnics   Lodge celebrations
    National and local holidays   Special local celebrations

XVII. Schools
    The buildings inside and out   The teachers
    The pupils—at work and at play—going to school
    Special schools   Consolidated school buses

XVIII. Homes
    A small but selected set of outside photographs of homes.
    Show the better home areas and the area where the poorer
    people live—show types of homes.
    Front yards—back yards
    Back porch—detail may be quite revealing—cutting lawn,
    picking flowers, raking and burning leaves—working
    in garden— lawn furniture and ornaments—washing
    out to dry.
    "Down by the tracks"
    Home gardens

A set of pictures inside of representative homes
Fittings—furniture, decorations, bric-a-brac, curtains,
pictures, mantels
Home in the evening—how do people spend their
evenings—show this at varied income levels
Eating— cooking
Dress-sewing—sewing machines
Listening to the radio   Bridge or other games
Playing with children   Care of baby
Parties—dinners—guests

XIX. Local Industry
    What keeps the town going?
    As far as the time permits, a study of local industries
    would be of great value.

XX. Utilities
    Water system   Light and Power
    Sewage disposal   Garbage disposal
    Telephone and Telegraph

XXI. Politics and Government
    Town meetings
    Campaigning—political rallies and parades,
    signs and placards
    Election day scenes—voting, standing around
    polling places

XXII. Miscellaneous
    Fires—going to fires   Fire bells, alarms, or signals
    Signs—traffic, welcome, service club, tourist,
    general signs
    Waste dumps
    Elevators in buildings (especially old ones)
    Delivery of newspapers
    People sitting on porch
    Women visiting on porch
    Women visiting "over backyard fence"
    Dogs running around streets
    The cemetery   Vacant lots
    Street peddlers   Unpaved streets—mud holes
    Alleys
    "The edge of town" where the town and country meet
    (a difficult thing to show)
    "Getting the mail"
    "Shack town"—try to get pictures of each town's "slum"
    Hitching racks for teams and horses (look on back streets).

Selected Bibliography

PHOTOGRAPHY

Hurley, F. Jack. *Portrait of a Decade: Roy Stryker and the Development of Documentary Photography in the Thirties.* Baton Rouge: Louisiana State University Press, 1972.

_____. *Russell Lee: Photographer.* Dobbs Ferry: Morgan and Morgan, 1978.

Louisville. University of Louisville. Roy Stryker Collection.

Morse, John D., ed. *Ben Shahn.* New York: Praeger Publishers, 1972.

O'Neal, Hank. *A Vision Shared: A Classic Portrait of America and Its People 1935-1943.* New York: St. Martin's Press, 1976.

Pratt, Davis, ed. *The Photographic Eye of Ben Shahn.* Cambridge: Harvard University Press, 1975.

Steichen, Edward, ed. *The Bitter Years, 1935-1941: Rural America as Seen by the Photographers of the Farm Security Administration.* New York: Museum of Modern Art, 1962.

Stryker, Roy Emerson, and Wood, Nancy. *In This Proud Land: America 1935-1943 as Seen in the FSA Photographs.* Greenwich: New York Graphic Society, 1973.

Washington, D.C. Archives of American Art. Correspondence. Roy Stryker. Microfilm.

_____. Interviews. Richard K. Doud with FSA Photographers. Transcribed.

Weiss, Margaret R., ed. *Ben Shahn Photographer: An Album from the Thirties.* New York: DaCapo Press, 1973.

HISTORY

Fairbanks, Robert B. "Cincinnati and Greenhills: The Response to a Federal Community, 1935-1939." *Cincinnati Historical Society Bulletin* 36 (1978): 223-41.

Lynd, Robert S., and Lynd. Helen. *Middletown: A Study in Contemporary American Culture.* New York: Harcourt, Brace, and Company, 1929.

Sternsher, Bernard. "Depression and New Deal in Ohio: Lorena A. Hickok's Letters to Harry Hopkins, 1934-36." *Ohio History* 86 (1977): 258-77.

_____. *Rexford Tugwell and the New Deal.* New Brunswick, N.J.: Rutgers University Press, 1964.

LITERATURE

Agee, James, and Evans, Walker. *Let Us Now Praise Famous Men.* Boston: Houghton Mifflin Co., 1941.

Anderson, Sherwood. *Hometown: The Face of America.* New York: Alliance Corp., 1940.

Caldwell, Erskine. *God's Little Acre.* New York: Viking Press, 1933.

_____. *Tobacco Road.* New York: Charles Scribner's Sons, 1932.

Conroy, Jack. *The Disinherited.* New York: Covici-Friede, 1933.

Dahlberg, Edward. *Bottom Dogs.* New York: Simon and Schuster, 1930.

Di Donato, Pietro. *Christ in Concrete.* New York: Bobbs-Merrill, 1937.

Dos Passos, John. *U.S.A..* New York: Harcourt, Brace, and Company, 1937.

Farrell, James T. *Studs Lonigan.* New York: Vanguard Press, 1935.

Gold, Mike. *Jews Without Money.* New York: Liveright, 1930.

Halper, Albert. *The Foundry.* New York: Viking Press, 1934.

Herbst, Josephine. *Pity Is Not Enough.* New York: Harcourt, Brace, and Company, 1933.

_____. *The Executioner Waits.* New York: Harcourt, Brace, and Company, 1934.

_____. *Rope of Gold.* New York: Harcourt, Brace, and Company, 1939.

Kazin, Alfred. *On Native Grounds: An Interpretation of Modern American Prose Literature.* New York: Reynal and Hitchcock, 1942.

Mumford, Lewis. *The Culture of Cities.* New York: Harcourt, Brace, and Company, 1938.

Steinbeck, John. *In Dubious Battle.* New York: Collier, 1936.

_____. *The Grapes of Wrath.* New York: Viking Press, 1939.

Stott, William. *Documentary Expression and Thirties America.* New York: Oxford University Press, 1973.

Twelve Southerners. *I'll Take My Stand.* New York: Harper and Brothers, 1930.

Vorse, Mary Heaton. *Strike!.* New York: Liveright, 1930.